Magical creatures or even weapons.
These are not the things
that make us really strong.
Or could it.
It's the courage to make mistakes
and to stand up for it.
True strength are honesty and humanity.
Accept it, like a human being.
Whether religion, colour or love for others.
To be there for each other,
The hand is enough to give confidence and love,
To get up again,
That is the true strength of each one.
And she's in each of us.
Because everyone has the same feelings,
efeels you in every way
that you can't be in a different way.
But the pain and joy are the same.
Like you & me.

1.
What do you have to do to gain trust?
Who does one have to be for someone else
to receive this?
Is it wrong to ask for trust?
I am me and show myself as I am.
I give you my hand in trust,
in what may come.

2.
the year is coming
the last rays of sun sink into the sea.
what remains
the memory
the pain you have inflicted on others
of a time when you're apart,
a time from which we learned
what should really matter.
the people we love
to accept everyone as they are
and to protect what Mother Nature has given us into our
hands.
Our life, their life... the life of every creature.
And so shines the new year,
with hope in my heart
with the first rays of sunshine of a new life,
another chapter
in which we learn
and what we learned
to pass on.

3.
They dance down in their white dress
glittering and bright,
it shines even in the night.
Gather in groups
floating and light,
soft as feathers.
Cover the bottom delicately.
the joyful smiles of the children,
shines the next day
while the world sleeps
under the quiet blanket of winter.

4.
Crunching every step in the snow,
walks you through the night.
Even the sounds of the cars
fall silent while driving
resemble the sneaking of cats.
in the light of the lantern,
Watch them shine from the falling stars.

5.
What is important,
is what you found in this life,
what you created.
you created new dreams
you live who you are
and share your heart,
a life,
which even for this moment,
may only be a dream
and will be one for the life to come.
Even if you or we forget
a part will remain
a dream in the heart.

6.
Today is your day,
even if for it for others
may be quite normal.
For us this is special
because today years ago
did you see the light of this world
lived your life
as you Like It,
to step by step
Feelings experienced positively and negatively.
We like to be with you
Whether near or far.
We don't want to miss you
because we like you too much.
Because you are this day
Because you are something special.

7.
Words are the most dangerous weapon in the world
which can destroy without violence
and just as much joy as love can bring.

Why are you hurting?
why are you destroying
Even though you don't want it.
Why is it so hard to heal
to conjure up a smile
bring joy to the eyes of others?
In moments when you're weak
and the world is sad
horrible
and is lonely.

It doesn't need words.
A gesture,
a sight,
a smile,
Can make the world shine again
and give warmth.

8.
Salute to the love of the country.
Show respect to his story
its people who built it.
Salute those who prepared your way
and show you respect for what you have created.
what you have achieved
because you are a part of it
what may come.

9.
My name is a mystery itself
I am the child of the moon
My heart is wild like the storm
What you see in my eyes
Free as the Wind,
and my passion is dangerous as fire.
My name is a mystery
long forgotten.
So give me a new name, my love.

10.
And we created a new universe.
where the sun and moon shine for us
and new life blossomed as a witness of our love.

11.
And if you believe that your heart
shattered by the wounds.
So there is someone
who sticks it together out of love,
or give you his.
while the other person
carries your heart in your chest.
So it connects you for a lifetime.

12.
Cut off from the people
working alone in his four walls.
Like trapped in a cage
with those you love and at the same time alone with
yourself.
want to escape
free yourself from invisible chains,
life again
as it was before
to live like this.
your inner desire
my wish,
Everyone's wish.
That's what it means to wait
escape into worlds of dreams,
which show us
how the future could be.
Designed by us
with the colors of our feelings,
for every creature we love.
Because the moment that remains
is the,
to save the energy to change something in the future.
with our colors
to reshape the world
which is now losing color
and may seem gray and dreary.

13.
Like stars sparkle her scales,
shine in the darkness of the deep.
No matter how deep you may lose yourself
between their desires
she gives you the star
that is for your wishes.
that star
who saves you from drowning
because you enlighten him
through your heart
your deepest wish.
And so he rises
and pulls you along
And gives you the strength
to fulfill her wish.

14.
Why do many say:
We were once children?
Aren't we anymore?
We are our parents' children.
We are children of the earth, of nature.
only now we hear
since we are adults
usually no longer.
Nevertheless we remain children
and still don't know much
we should listen
to learn.
We should never lose the child in us.
'Cause when that happens
we're just society dolls
and the world falls silent and remains sad.

15.
what you see
are signs of violence.
The smile
hide the shards of the soul.
If you try to put your heart together inside,
to let your own light shine more brightly.
But all alone?
just say thank you
for those who believe in me.
Thanks to those who support me.
Thank you for being there.
Because for you the colors I paint are
the words I write.
So that you are never alone in the dark.

16.
A mood staged,
raging inside everyone.
Just silently accepted
chained to mood,
against it pulls and fights,
while the body is at rest.
But she cannot be suppressed
fights the chains,
want to be free
wants to see the light.
If with time
spends in captivity
a tornado of savagery and fury emanates.

17.
what do you want with my heart
experience the wildness with me,
live through the dreams with me
and we create our own magic,
in the untamed world of you and me.
Because you are my heart.

18.
the heat burns
burns the body
tingles on the skin
it awakens the fire of passion,
what I feel for you.
do you see the flickering glow
in my opinion?

19.
look in my eyes
in the brown of the earth
see the red of the wild soul.
Do you accept the wolf?
do you accept my protection?
Will you take my hand when I give it to you?
Or do you deny me who I am
like I am,
just because i'm different?
Then open your eyes
because no one is like the other.
there are more like me
each soul in a different form,
in another body.

20.
The brush glides over the white fabric,
spread the colors
which arises from feelings.
Dive into the gray of the world
and gives her color
distributes them to the world.
'Cause we color them,
create a new world
a rainbow of our feelings.

21.
you will never get lost
if you remember me.
to my voice,
to my laughter.
Close your eyes
and remember me,
because then you can always see me.
'Cause I'm a part of your heart,
a part of your dreams.

22.
Her gaze is longingly directed to the sea,
the clouds hang grey,
heavy oppress the heart.
That heart waiting for the light
the warmth that gently tickles the skin,
the heart filled with happiness and hope,
hope for the future,
the love... that is longingly waiting for you somewhere.

23.
Even when you're feeling down
even when you think the pain is overwhelming.
You are not alone,
because we are by your side
the people who love you
who protect you
who support you.
We never leave you alone.
So be happy and laugh
because you conquer the darkness
with the light of your heart.

24.
My heartbeat will never stop
to beat for your words
for your feelings
in every word
your passion
in every sentence
your heart,
which one with your poems,
keeps on beating for eternity.

25.
Embark on the dangerous adventure
take the risk
I promise you,
You will not regret it,
because I promise you
I'll show you a world full of dreams.
An adventure with dormant thoughts,
like old tales of dragons,
who slumber in the mountains,
whose fire is so hot
like longing for you

26.
the gleam in the eyes,
created by tears.
you are no shame
no reason to be ashamed.
No tears of pain
but tears of gratitude.
Especially for those
who otherwise experience no gratitude,
One word can touch the heart
the tears flow.
Because the warmth fills the heart
the cracks in the soul
make it disappear.

27.
When gratitude makes you cry.
what happened to the people?
If the honesty
touches you with a warm voice,
and you feel helpless.
Why are you afraid to believe?
A human,
who trusted others
because he hoped not to be alone
and believed lies
heals the shards of his broken soul
And yet never gives up.
to make others happy and to be honest,
so they don't experience the same pain
and get lost in the dark
a strength that is rare.

28.
the gleam in the eyes,
through tears of joy.
a heart that touches
through warm words.
The smile looks sad
and yet full of honesty,
because it is grateful
for something,
which the person rarely experiences.

29.
if your world
tears itself apart
shows a broken mirror.
When the human by your side
pick up shard by shard,
your heart,
joins your soul
this is love
for infinity
conquering all darkness.

30.
no matter what happens
never give up hope
Enjoy the moment,
in the here and now.
Don't take anything for granted
neither others nor yourself.
You are special and always will be
no matter what happens
those who love you
for them you will be immortal.
So enjoy
laugh,
dream and fight.
stay as you are
in the here and now
because that is something for you and for us,
the most important is.

31.
looking up at the stars,
enjoy the rest of the night.
listen to the whisper of the wind,
until the moment
when the warm rays
of the golden light awakens.
caress your hair,
kisses your cheeks
let the warmth inside you
fills you with happiness.

32.
filled with warmth,
of love,
Of luck.
I'm missing you,
In thought,
In the distance,
you are far away from me
But I'm a part of you
Like you from me.
carry you with me
Very close,
In the now and here.

33.
If I were an island
Somewhere in the sea.
If I were your refuge
In the stormy time.
While darkness eats you away
overpower the waves
That you lose yourself in it.
is my country
protective,
I hold you in my arms

34.
Even with gray clouds
don't let it spoil your mood.
also the rain
brings new life
and wipe away the negative thoughts.
so that your own light
like the hope
as the sun shines.

35.
She saw,
how souls come and go
in every part of nature
into every creature.
She saw,
the magic of love,
The life.

36.
paths woven like a web,
chosen from the beginning of time.
Elected since we make choices
to find our way
Inseparable,
but go away
those ways
which we do not choose.
No matter where you lead
we hope,
they bring us to the goal
which we wish.
If we walk a path
the others disappear into the darkness.
so choose wisely
You can't turn back and change your mind
your way to destiny

37.
Your way,
Your destiny.
your life not alone
because he is woven
with those you meet.
those you leave
those whose life you step into.
But only you decide
which way you go.

38.
music sounds,
sensual and gentle.
tender touches,
wander over her body.
its warmth,
tickles her skin,
awakens the passion
after him.
As in a dream.

39.
a blink of an eye,
who rekindled.
the world of words,
like a storm
nourished by the feelings
through the spirit.
born of truth
tears the world apart
and yet in the heart
united by the poet.

40.
So he climbs out
from the pitch-black sea.
which devoured him
silenced him
like a thousand others.
only the storm of feelings drowns them out,
those who are silent in the sea
until they find the strength
to ascend
So he progresses
naked,
yet clothed in truth.
An armor indestructible,
and yet rare.
appears through the light,
which he carries in his heart.

41.
floating in the dark,
quiet and yet infinitely loud.
echoes the heart's echo,
afraid of being forgotten.
Carried on their own wings of light,
and yet she falls down.
reaching for love,
which you hoped
in vain,
and yet you don't give up.

42.
consider
no matter where you are.
your joy and your sorrow,
every person feels
no matter where he is.
souls,
invisible lights,
not visible to everyone
accompany our way.
connect with others,
no matter where you are.
even if you fall
one is never alone
because everyone knows the feeling.
And everybody,
can be of help.
others are shadows
who support
mostly not visible
connected in heart.
So hold on to the people
close to you,
who will help you as well.
Never lose sight
what luck you have experienced
keep it in your heart
give some of it back to the world.

43.
As you read these words
is a part of me with you.
stand behind you
protect you.
keeps the shadows away from you,
because your heart is too precious.
Your light shines even brighter.
So I ask you:
laugh, be happy and fight,
Don't hide.

44.
a mute child,
a soul destroyed.
The innocence does not know
why she deserves the pain.
the urge to protect
but the body is still so small
calls you silently for help,
she asks those
to see her pain
to take pity on her.

45.
do you hear them sing
the old songs?
renew the faith
dancing around the fire
shapes from dreams,
from fantasy
and the spirit.
creatures that play
they dance
and we,
who delight in your spirit.
'Cause you're all around us
of flower, tree,
born of air, fire and earth.

46.
the heart flutters,
at his gaze.
She lowers her eyes
but he does not retreat.
He takes her in his arms
she enjoys his scent.
A reminder of the moment
a tender kiss.

47.
The year is coming to an end
drags the gray time with it.
We say goodbye to you with family,
with friends.
Say goodbye with a kiss
hope for a better time
let's say goodbye with this poem.
past go away
but you taught us a lot
we now know even more
what we have to appreciate.
Let's not forget that.
Now we hold
what is dear to us,
nothing that can be weighed with money,
family, friends, health,
the moment,
You and me.

48.
Let's Dance,
tonight in dreams.
Let's dance between the sirens
who sing a song for us.
A dance for eternity
a dance between sun and moon,
which will not end.

49.
gray and dreary,
it's all around her.
sad and bald
like the season
this is how she feels.
But when a warmth tickles her,
gently caresses her face,
a smile appears
new strength is born.

50.
Swords clash vibratingly at each other,
a world is created in front of her inner eye.
born of words
she roams the sky
she travels the world.
a heart full of courage
plunges you into another world.
In reality it is not noticeable.
Here she is heard
here she is seen.
Here she can just be herself.

51.
eyes drop,
the soul travels the world.
In thought,
in spirit,
to protect those.
help them with words
not to let those fall into the darkness.
with the people
to share the power
to find their own strengths.
To let hope shine again.

52.
run!
Run towards your goal.
grasp the goal,
what you long for in your heart.
We'll all meet again there
and walk the path together.

53.
Fallen does not mean lost.
The moment that pulls you down
passes.
as long as you fall
never look down.
keep an eye on the light
keep the hope in your heart,
the shadows pass,
take you back to a world,
full of love and warmth,
a world without pain.

54.
every beat of the music,
awakens a new feeling.
is pulled along
lets us remember what was.
Let's see what is
of moments filled with sorrow,
with moments touched by a smile.
With every beat of this music
everyone has their own song
the song of falling,
the song of strength
the song of life
The music of the heart.

55.
what is born of pain
won't always live in the shadows.
what is born of pain
will rise to the light.
It's what we make of it
we just can't give up.
Don't give the darkness a chance
and lose yourself in her
we lose hope
we lose our faith
to all of us, to you and me.

56.
rest at the end,
where our future is.
earth cold and dark,
we become a part of you.
Where we are going?
This is uncertain
but also in that place
we will never be alone
those who came before us
also went this way.
But what counts
is what you do
what you can do
in the here and now.

57.
a dance in his arms,
like a dream long ago.
A moment in the past
in a white dress.
passion and love,
outlast the time
which runs
like sand through our fingers.
Two again at the moment.
not to be without him
the wish,
the moment would last
dance the dance again
for several years.

58.
a covenant of eternity,
who unites two souls
outlasts time.
In life,
as well as afterwards.
a love,
which reveals itself.
Even if you don't find each other,
in the crowds of souls
one will be reborn at some point.
a chance again
in the world to touch
to find the way again.
to walk the path again
together.

59.
words,
which are born of desires.
to experience them once
not lost hope yet.
to reach for
carrying this in the heart,
the struggle of life
to get through
the fight,
to fulfill these.

60.
This world is not a dream.
It consists not only of light,
but most of the time we don't see the shadows.
We don't want to see you
hide in deep within us.
But we too
consist of shadow and light.
Our heart shows us
our feelings.
It's the truth,
about you and me
so don't ignore them.

61.
Silent screams,
tears that flow.
locked in a room
ignored by those
those should love she.
caused her the pain
and left you alone with it.
Why can't this world be loving?

62.
pieces of soul,
drift like islands,
in the sea of feelings
In the spirit,
in the heart,
filled with memories
cut the wounds.
Not visible from the outside.
Can you see these
with a look in the eye?

63.
a breath in the night
born with an oath.
draws the soul into the night,
her memory of past lives,
long lost.
just knowing what she is
no matter what its shell looks like now.
She roams the dreams of souls,
which has protected you for centuries.
Those who get their oath
spread out over the world.
Are you the one who hears you calling?
But on the day
the form, not so like the soul.
No memory of last night
to the fight
to protect others
the fight against the shadow realm.

64.
devoured by hate,
of sadness and pain.
Do you feel lost
is heavy on your heart.
If you don't know,
find no way out
you feel alone

Are you giving up?
No!

'Cause this is a part
this is the resume.
Never give up.
hold on to you
you can move something.
stand by yourself
follow your goals.
This is your life.
So get up!

65.
we are warriors
we are fighters.
we are healers
we are guardians.
we are small
and yet big.
we act alone
and yet they are not.
We cause harm and pain
build and destroy.
We are who we are,
despite wounds in spirit and soul,
we help others
and go unnoticed
our ways together.

66.
"Stay as you are!"
I will not forget these words.
you will always be a part of me
because you never wanted
that I bend
that I am like others.
I kept that promise.
To find those
who see me the same
accept and understand me.
I'm looking for these people
but I know one thing.
you watch over us all
I won't forget that.

67.
the heart beats wildly,
filled with adventures.
new worlds arise
sprung from the pen
fills the pages of the book.
Gives new life to the blank pages
a world to draw the reader in,
to be a part of something
to give strength and dreams
to dive through the seas
And fly through the sky.

68.
plunge into a sea,
from deep darkness.
a silence
screaming infinitely loud.
Our hearts echo so loud
with every beat
suddenly images appear.
in the darkness around us,
every picture a memory.
sinking down,
get lost.
But with renewed courage
let's get some air
brought to life.
Awakened with new strength.

69.
we decide
who we are.
who we want to be
have been following this since they were little.
Losing sight to be happy
to set no expectations
and free us from our doubts.
we make decisions
what comes after
we cannot steer.
We should not only think of ourselves
but also think of others.
reaches out to each other,
without having any expectations.
easy to help
life will do the rest.

70.
Her power was once so great
everyone knew her name.
She gave you the strength to get up
Goals,
no matter how difficult they were
were won like a victory.
She is still there today
but most lose their sight
no longer hear your words.
But let's give her back her power.
By believing in them.
keep she in our hearts
the hope
who gave us the strength
to endure everything.

71.
In her own
small world
Don't live alone in your thoughts.
retreats into
And hopes that the people
that she thinks of
who she doesn't even know
just being happy.
Even if it can't be right now.

72.
I am the black wolf
who walks through the darkness.
The white blemish in my fur
located there
where my heart beats and lies.
the shape of wings,
almost angelic,
I go to those
who lost themselves
from sadness, pain and loneliness,
to the dark realm.
I am the guard
that you can't see in the dark.
The soul fighting for you
who believes in you
and has a different shape in reality.

73.
a brushstroke,
paint on a blank wall.
arises a world
from a different point of view.
a world of desires,
who still speaks the truth
because the heart shows
like the world for the artist
really is.

74.
Feelings are not there to be hidden.
show your tears
don't be ashamed of that.
show your smile
when you are happy
and let your light shine.
There is no need to be ashamed of feelings.
you are right the way you are
because you are unique.
Something special.
You are a miracle to your family
a present for your friends
and you are a reminder for those to come.

75.
lost in the dark
not seeing the light.
tearing the loneliness
you approach blindly.
falls down,
loses hope and happiness
but open your heart
learn to trust, because that gives you wings,
brings you back to the light.
'Cause fear is a part
that you don't need to fear
you are never alone,
because others feel just like you
Because others have fears too.

76.
Appearance is just a mask
a shine.
To please society.
your real face
is your soul
it is the light within you.
only the people
who really see
can in your eyes
see inside you
see the world with your eyes
don't pay attention to the mask
but on your soul.
They pay attention to your light.

77.
In a world of sand and stone
no sea
not a drop of water.
no green,
that can live in the heat
that burns me
from the inside out.
are you my hope
my shadow
who protects me.
my source
that never runs dry
you me with your love,
filled with new life.

78.
to see what grows
his life is on its way.
Like a tree,
developed a strength
and step by step
goes his own way
struggle through life.
It makes you proud
to see this life.
Because that's how you know
i can go in peace

79.
We learn in life
since the beginning of time.
the earth observes
any birth.
Our mother,
our origin
accompanies a lifetime
drawn in nature,
in the form of our planet,
an ancient goddess,
long forgotten
takes us invisibly by the hand.
But what do we give you back?
Except our body
when we die
Is that lucky for her?

80.
shadows consume one,
Thoughts sink into the darkness.
a life
that thinks and feels
that it will be forgotten.
society that forms
an image emerges
if you don't adapt
in the here and now
becomes invisible to everyone.

So develop the power
stand out from the world
no matter how different you are.
There is always someone
the this side
accepted and loved.
who supports you
and sticks by you.

81.
passion and courage,
united in heart.
A fire that must never be extinguished
no matter how dark it seems.
it in everyone
so light up the world
With your deeds and words
until the light
combined with that of billions.

82.
blow after blow,
endure the pain.
suffering in the heart
invisible the scars.
tears which have not been seen
hide what is happening.
the body rises,
in pain,
a power blossoms
do you fight
through the inner darkness
and hope for the light.

83.
Reach for what lies ahead
hold on to it.
a crystal,
that turns into a rose.
a sky,
which turns red.
A dream,
who comes to life.
Your dream,
Your life,
that takes shape through you.

84.
he grabs his sword
fighting for you
who waits in the distance.
The ones you haven't seen in a long time.
But how long had this been happening?
His heart,
hasn't been beating for a long time.
His eyes,
looking longingly into the distance.
The heart that rests
and after life still fights,
and love is looking for

85.
flakes fall down,
Small crystals gleaming in the light.
playing with the sunlight
dancing in the wind,
ring like bells,
magic to the children,
A smile on your face.
forms creatures,
Born from the imagination.
Live in another world
As long as the ground is frozen.
comes the sun
with its warming rays,
her shape disappears
live on,
In another world.

86.
Everyone searches in their own way
Something that makes him happy.
according to material values,
Will be thought of first.
Look into your heart and be honest with yourself
what you really want
Can't be bought.
it is a person
One hand,
Which is reaching for you.

87.
words,
which cut into the heart.
Hands,
that cause pain.
Lonely,
sitting in a room.
searching,
after the question:
Why did this happen?
years that have passed
a heart wounded
hurt a soul.
But never give up in life
to learn,
to find happiness
and keep it in your heart.

88.
The darkness,
seems so quiet and mute.
But listen carefully
hear the screams in it.
feelings,
hidden in the shadows.
the monsters inside
are not monsters.
people who suffer
don't push them away.
give you a hand
lead you into the light
help you bear this pain
put a smile on their face.

89.
War,
born of desire.
Born of greed.
a call for help,
in the time now and here.
people who suffer
tears are shed
lives which end.
words of happening,
recorded in books.
What will the future think about it?

90.
warm rays of the sun,
tickle the skin.
songs around,
Nature awakens.
a hand gesture,
a shimmer,
flies with the wind.
where it arises
nature blooms again.
A tree,
a flower,
spring wins over gray time.

91.
a look into the distance,
the longing awakens.
to explore this world
not only at night.
to fight for dreams
never to forget these.
to fulfill they
to make our world more colorful
this is at our discretion.

92.
To be happy,
is important in a gray time.
just for yourself alone,
it shouldn't be like that.
to feel happiness
by acting for yourself
does not bring true happiness.
Help,
watch after,
be by someone's side
to see his smile.
Someone in hard times
be with one
to help him up and to see him smile.
the warmth we feel
this is how true happiness should be.

93.
Today the silence is unbearable
even during the day.
No rest screams like that
moderate
like the end
a section,
of a life tone.

94.
shadows of people
are not the wounds of the soul.
shadow of emotions
caused by action
are creatures
pulling you into the dark.
rob you of your hope
and devour your light.
So never give up
To fight against these shadows.

95.
fear of falling,
into the darkness
loneliness.
Not chosen voluntarily
the path is rich with tears.
pushed by those
who was trusted.

96.
I do not give up hope,
I go my way.
The way to the light.
Even if I stumble
even if i fall
Ain't the dark my way
because the pain
which tugs at me inside.
who wants to prevent me
to go forward.
I won't let it stop me
keep fighting,
just be selfish
just feel lucky.
this is my way
following the warmth
guided by the light
my eyes fixed on it.
Feel this light just once.

97.
A storm is coming,
wild the feelings.
But I don't feel fear
because my heart is in turmoil
it wants the truth
see who is in the eye of the storm.

98.
she walks towards him
reaches for him.
Holds the longing
after his proximity.
He ignores her presence
does not see her longing.
Don't turn around.
Because the moment
that they shared
was just the moment.
So her hand lowers
her memory remains.

99.
a flash,
a shadow.
A figure in the dark.
eyes that shine
lusts for the light
yearns for you
feeds on the pain
want you to be one of them.
So hope and trust
get up and run!
your light is your weapon
before the shadows.
the belief in you
is the light of your soul
of your heart.

100.
crying eases the pain
which the heart carries with it.
tears are the result
which reveals longing and pain.
wipe away the tear
when you see them.
remove the burden
which is on the heart.
Only if you mean it honestly
feel strong
to share the suffering.
Otherwise the next tear,
be the result of your actions.

101.
she gave you her hand
faced the suffering
which she herself experienced in the background.
protecting from the figures,
with a grimacing face.
protects a child
another being.
Bearing your courage like a sword
in the heart the light.
not realizing
that the blade of treachery,
behind him,
stabs.

102.
her thoughts with him.
Wandering into the distance.
Humming an unknown melody
tenderly the wind takes her away.
on the long way
where he is
in a strange place.
lets the wind
through leaves and grass,
her song sound.
and his heart
sing inside.

103.
wings splendor,
covered with feathers.
old creatures,
so holy
are born of light
a new being is awakened by every birth.
see in good,
like in bad times
after us anytime.
laugh with us
support us.
But is it clear to us
we speak of loneliness.
That is not true,
because these beings are always there.

104.
a colorful world
with mythical creatures.
A world of shadows
and light,
recorded on paper,
born in fantasy
come alive in the heart.

105.
Swords clink in the wind,
carry a plaintive song.
A song of pain and sadness
between calls for love and freedom.
attacks the knight
already injured by the war
after his sword.
full of longing,
fighting for those
to whom he reveals his heart.

106.
her eyes closed
darkness around them.
she stretches out her hand
the light of her soul rises up.
illuminates the darkness
shows a landscape
rich and beautiful.
a night so bright
in the silver glow.
awakening other souls,
emerge
and invite you to dance.

107.
petals rise,
form a robe.
the dance of spring,
has the heart of winter in his hand.
spellbound his gaze
is he so close to her
but their bright colors
would oust him.
so gray and sad
not worthy enough
to court her.
she takes his hand
at the beginning of May.
the only touch
where all spirits are unbound and free.

108.
guard born,
with shadow and light.
Look like you and me
Shapes of your souls can be different,
the being, however, formed by life,
will be the same as ours.
born to live
to protect,
to suffer and feel pain.
they will
protect you in a wondrous way.
support you,
touch your heart and soul.

109.
look in your hand
clench them into a fist.
keep your pain in
which is heavy on your heart.
open your hand
and let it out.
you don't have to wear it
silent and still.
strength is
to show feelings
not to keep in secret.
'Cause this isn't real
what you want

110.
Born in the sign of Leo
between sun and moon,
comes to life.
carrying the soul of the wolf,
bathed in fire,
between courage and suffering.
Decorated with scars on the inside,
united in spirit with nature,
with every step
free himself from the darkness.

111.
step by step,
leaves footprints in the sand.
waves carry them away
like she was never there
to an unknown place.
Just the wind and the tide
tell about her
who left their mark
with the unknown song
which nobody ever plays.

112.
I know you are here
after a long time
and yet unforgettable.
maybe I'll hold you
like a chain to me.
Don't let yourself be pulled or let go.
Were you the one who accepted me
the one,
who saw the truth.
don't be afraid of me
don't judge me to be different
Please stay here a little longer.
Please stay by my side.
I promise,
I let your soul go
i release you

113.
wise companion,
you lie there in silence.
constantly paying attention
are you there for me
a beast,
a heart so true
turn around
seem to ignore me
but you are always near
when I am sad.
you are by my side
and in my heart
always there.

114.
to travel into space in your sleep,
Between the Stars
Accompanied by friends and family.
discover worlds,
passes time and space,
to visit distant stars,
until now
A dream.

115.
looking at the moon,
in thoughts with you.
as far away
my heart travels to you.
looking to the sky,
do you see him like me
Even if time passes differently.
Do you ever see him like me?
So he carries my tears
full of longing for you.
The wind carries the warmth
that envelops you in the evening,
like a blanket
my love in heart
who longs for you.

116.
A knight,
explores the world.
a warrior,
with magical power,
protecting your friends.
A witch,
who only wants good.
A king,
who rules wisely with the heart.
a world full of dreams
love and happiness.
qualities that vanish
as a child we are these characters,
fighting for peace.

117.
All around only darkness
around you only fear and suffering.
hands on ears,
tries to deaden the voices
that cause suffering and pain.
holding hands in front of eyes
not to see
what people carry with them.
Even thoughts hurt
don't show others
his inner pain and his own suffering.
So you feel left alone
alone with pain and suffering,
the inner voices that only hate you,
but you are never really alone.

118.
open your eyes
see the path ahead of you.
open your ears
to hear the voices
who want to help you.
Open your heart,
and let the light in.
Because it drives away the loneliness and fear,
because you are not alone.
that's nobody
if you just look closely.
reaches out to each other,
help and listen.
This is how volumes are built for life.

119.
Millions of people,
on this planet.
million creatures,
over time.
give a take
a come and go.
This is the cycle
in life.

120.
Travel,
discover the world.
touch the sand
from distant countries.
A desire,
a dream,
make him real
because your life is just this,
You only experience it once.

121.
No matter how the darkness gnaws at you
your grief tears you apart
the loneliness grabs you.
you come out
through your strength
through your light
grab it,
don't pretend.

122.
ice in the heart,
the blood froze.
born of old legends
the giants brood.
a creature of legends,
a secret in the ice,
the dragon creature,
consisting of spoil and bones.

123.
you see my smile
do you see the pain too?
Do you know my scars
which carries my soul.
caused by humans
I hide the fear
to be dropped
like it always was
As if I were just an object.
But call it stupid
call it naive
I do not want to give up.
to find people
who accept me
who I am.

124.
she kneels down
into the fresh wet.
Waves gently caress your legs.
She runs her hand over the clear surface.
a carpet of stars,
above and below her.
Only she shines in the middle.
A young lady,
with fiery red hair
and the azure
in her eyes.
her soul shines,
her heart burns
and let life flourish.

125.
Support is not common
not generally to everyone
it's not constant.
Support does not start
in fame and power.
It shouldn't be like that.
It's a decision
of people to help someone
of the heart.
It should be honest.

can support this
gestures and words,
start with the person next to you.
It can help everyone
because it shows
who is behind you

Support does not start
when you have achieved something.
It's words you say
and things you do
You don't only get support from people you love,
friends or family,
but also strangers in the moment of time.
It's the things you love
which one only sees over time,
shows a relationship invisibly.

So the support should not be covered with shadows,
neither with hatred, attention and envy.

If this is noticeable
the other person.
This is how you sow your own suffering.
and sometimes the loneliness.

Because who you support
shake hands
accept this
a bit of trust in you
gives a piece of his heart.

So think
who you support
Because this also shows a lot of courage.

126.
Your thoughts
create worlds.
Your dreams
become true.
So fight
for your dreams
To reach your goal.
'Cause it's never wrong
to live for it.

127.
She sings in her world
she dances in the most beautiful dress.
On the sea,
which acts like a mirror.
in the colors of nature,
does she achieve that
what they do in our world
not reached.
Because she lost
the confidence in herself.

128.
step by step
the dream goes with you.
beg you
not to ignore him
to withdraw from him.
asks you
not to give up on him.
Did you believe in him for so long
but you lose your courage
and the strength to endure
is slowly being stolen from him.
until there is nothing left of him
has meaning and
in the shadows to the silly
memories will.

129.
Best friends are not found overnight.
The time will tell,
the time will come.
they are human
who share a lot.
Through thick and thin,
a band
one Love,
on the same level
connected by time and hearts.

130.
lying on a beach,
with black sand.
Ash,
gently rocking slides down,
like snowflakes in winter,
down to the body.
Lying between shards and sand,
cut light scratches into the skin.
sweeps the arm across the floor,
at the touch of those shards,
a memory awakens.

131.
Softly she dreams of him
dances with him on a lake,
so mirror like.
Sun and moon,
even the stars
dance with you.
You lost him so long ago
but the memory remains
for even death does not divide love.

132.
bells are ringing,
nature sleeps and dreams.
Covered under the white blanket
and now draws new strength.
The mother who sleeps
her children wrapped in the blanket.
only the guard children
they play in the snow
monitor the time
enjoy gifts,
other spirits and beings.
long forgotten and yet always there,
the mother,
she so bright full of splendor,
a variety of colors,
awakened in the world.

133.
An angel born as a human
chosen for protection without wings.
looks up to you,
eyes light up in all colors,
yours so same.
If you see the suffering he experiences as a human being,
and yet not giving up.
'Cause you're a person
which this angel protects.
No matter how far away you are
no matter what he looks like.
he protects you
and maybe you ignore him
don't see him.
But the angel is there
stands behind you
and gives you his hand.
gives you his courage
part of his love
and his power.

134.
One World,
so dark around
Mirrors appear and shatter.
in the shards the images of life.
pictures of joy,
which you are trying to put together.
images of suffering,
whirling around in the chaos of feelings,
and cut wounds in the skin.
Just an image of the soul
Wounds not visible on the outside
but if you look straight in the eye.
sinking into the depths of the gaze,
so this world of man sees.

135.
diving and swimming,
in the freedom of the sea.
every fish
every creature
a mystery.
Welcome you gently into your world.
No fear,
because you are a part of it too.
Because for them you are
also a mystery
only you can change your world
not enter and not see properly.

136.
every creature
born in this world.
looks up at the stars,
and wonders
what the meaning of his life is.
Has a purpose?
Do I have to do something specific?
No matter what happens in life
whether good or bad
they are things
that make you.
You don't have to do anything specific.
Just be yourself.
create your own world
the way you want to see them.
with the person
with which you are connected.
Begin your adventure
in your co-created world.
The purpose of you being there
that you should live.

137.
A little boy,
always sees a figure of light in a dream.
she takes care of him
she dances with him.
She wipes away his tears.
When the boy grows up
he only sees her from time to time.
'Cause he's losing faith in you
he loses faith in dreaming.
But the feeling
which awakens you in Him,
remains.
his heart beats faster
a heat awakens the body.
His desire to see your face
gets bigger year by year.
The more the longing grows
so little does it appear in dreams.
As long as he searches in his world
until he finds the feeling again
and finally holds you in his arms.

138.
She covers her ears
wants to escape the noise.
Her mother's accusations
the man's threats
who is supposed to be her father.
silent in the room
looks at the sky.
Beg the gods old
and those who have been forgotten
that it will be peaceful
that she no longer has to fear anything.
She listens to herself
just the beating of her heart.
The fear so great
the noise outside only gets louder.
Opens the door
and step out into the light
against fear and pain,
just to protect the one
that brought you into this world.

139.
falling of an angel,
battle scars,
cover his body.
When falling, the body burns in the light,
the once golden hair
the white wings.
Now so black
that it swallows the darkness.
feathers scattered around the body,
where he stands
Shows only the blue of her eyes
the warmth and cold of the kingdom of heaven.

140.
My blade is the pen
every word a wound
and a work of art at the same time.
A new world born
awakens a new life
gets them in your consciousness,
realized their full potential.

141.
Her voice rings out after a long time
a song so unknown
awakened from the depths of your heart.
A melody so new
the wind carries them away with joy.
Even if the song only sounds once,
and falls into oblivion.
So she found the courage
after a long forgotten time
to let her voice ring out
away from her
to a distant place.

142.
deep asleep in the mountain,
a skin like a shell.
The earth trembles at its rumble.
A volcano rises
when he spits his flames towards the sky.
Forget,
only a myth wrestles around him.
A being,
so equal to the mountain in its strength,
it withstands heat and cold.
Once heaven was rich.
hunted and feared
did he protect and guard
what he loves
a wrong picture
was given to him
now in the books
and lives in the hearts of men.
An ancient guardian of time
lives for eternity.

143.
she stands by the sea
the wind plays with her hair.
eyes closed,
she listens to the waves
who carry the song of the wind with them.
she raises her head
opens the dark gaze.
whispers to the wind
the oath that she will protect those
which mean something to her.
Wherever they are.

144.
A lake,
reflects the darkness of the night.
He devours the moon and the stars in it.
from the setting moon,
a shadowy figure rises.
Your gaze loving and warm,
but their clothes cold and dark.
If she hands you a crystal clear card,
you accept with a questioning look.
the stranger disappears with the moon,
and the sun brings the lake to life.
Makes the map shine
what you can read on it:
Fate.
because only you hold it in your hands.

145.
A buzz
like in a dream from afar.
it comes to you
with the wind from another country.
a flower of the desert,
a fairy of summer,
sings for you
you can sleep
sweet and gentle,
far from the dark.

146.
That's how I think of you
almost day by day.
Miss you,
a pain that won't go away.
words unspoken,
in the heart there
speak her softly whisper,
so only you can hear them.
so it hurts me
not having said it
when you sat by my side
gave me the strength
being me,
you were the human
who accepted me
as i was

so you are a part
for eternity
Not from my blood
but my family
someone by my side

147.
the hand caresses the flame,
feels her warmth but no pain.
reflected in the eyes
as she dances in the wind.
A creature so delicate
so distinctive and warm
can this flame
devour one,
in her tender and equally cruel arm.

148.
your gaze wanders over the words,
lets you travel to another world.
makes you feel
what others feel
lets you understand
what really matters.
makes you forget for a moment
what is happening in our world.
create your own
new courage awakens in you,
a strength that you take on
from the world from the book.
your strengthened being,
your new insight
carry into this world.

149.
the song is new
yet so well known.
caresses your heart
very soft.
love and hope,
Hand in hand,
is what the world needs
not only today,
not only now
but every moment
no matter where you are,
Day after day.

150.
tears that flow
don't be afraid to show them.
shed tears,
allow it
tears run dry,
like the pain in your chest.
what you wear
to ease your heart
tear for tear,
makes it easier to bear.

151.
A guard kneels
looks at the apparently lifeless body.
Feel it beat so weak
the spirit is still awake in it.
A whisper barely audible
this is how it gets into you:
"Live as you are
don't trust the fake sunshine!
Darkness is pure seduction
what you promise
is just a world of illusion.
Show your scars!
stand by it!
Don't wear your mask
throw them down
show them your wounds
because they have you
to the person
standing here now."

152.
my thoughts are floating
at that moment
when we met
memories long ago
built a life
laughed and cried.
led me into the light
if I'm lost
in the dark.
Our love is the music
to which our hearts dance.
a song for eternity
an oath
never to leave you
No matter where I am,
no matter what happens.
even in eternity
our hearts find each other
through our song.

153.
Feelings are rarely mentioned
pronounced,
what moves you.
Why all this?
When the world is crying
break relationships,
for this very reason
so you save yourself the suffering.
Why are we making it so difficult for ourselves?
The heart is already crying enough
feelings are worth
to be pronounced.
It requires and shows a lot of courage.

154.
Strength
to show his scars
to stand by his feelings.
With a straight look
to see into the future.
Even if your gaze falls,
don't lose yourself in the deep
the dark sea of your feelings
Don't look back at the wounds
which you inflicted.
stand by it
still go ahead.
I know it's hard
and it's hard to find out.
But someone shakes your hand
holds you when the pain is too much.
hold that person
even if it gets lost
and don't let go of each other.
Because the strength
that you previously owned alone,
is now infinitely large for two.

155.
Millions of people live on earth
We see billions of stars in the sky.
if one falls
a wish is born.
A child is born
to a being
that like everyone else thinks
brought up for it.
But if this child
raises his gaze to the sky,
is there a wish maybe.
If you had another being
maybe lived a different life?

156.
For your way a sound sounds,
your heart sets the pace
your life is the rhythm
The melody,
goes up and down.
full of bright tones,
it sounds with joy
the deep tones
full of sadness and pain.
But watch the beat
that he doesn't pass.
take care of your heart

157.
listening to the rain
that takes away the heat.
The cool air brings with it.
like a new section
who brings new life
who washes away the old
and the world blossoms again.

158.
a year goes by
with time as if in flight.
just lived
the grave calls for you.
But where is the time
that one still has?
Where have the years gone
that passed so quickly?
An instant,
a blink of an eye.
the years
the moments like lightning,
appear and show what was.

159.
A drop of ink
falls on the white sheet.
Runs carried by a gust of wind,
over the lifeless substrate.
runs along,
what opposes him
until its last drop of liquid
dried up in the leaf.
To the surprise of the artist,
gives a new picture.

160.
I hold my soul in my hands
bright with many cracks.
splinters fine as sand,
through my hands.
Shards reflect memories
which cut into the flesh.
with every piece
which my broken soul crumbles,
I feel the darkness
which reaches for my heart.
Look down at the heap
try to find the courage
to put them back together
to the blade against the darkness.

161.
A sea of red flowers
no roses,
timid and fine,
like the thread of life.
as red as the blood
which pulls
like a river its course.
A wind rocks her gently to and fro,
gentle and beautiful.
during the storm
snatches the petals from them,
bears her seed away,
grows and draws its line,
like veins along the earth.

162.
My gaze swept over the people
who pass by.
So different and yet the same.
your thoughts so different
but basically the same intention.
the most diverse desires,
but the same feelings.
As different as the dreams
but somewhere the hearts beat
in one beat
in the same pulse of time.

163.
I do not remember,
of my dreams from last night.
I do not remember,
to the colors
which they wear.
Be it light or shadow.
I remember something
a very long time ago.
a creature,
which she repressed
and when messenger appeared to me
for what he took from me afterwards.
Even today he shows
his eyes empty
with a sly grin on his face.
The messenger,
that promises fear and suffering.

164.
souls,
bound in chains.
shadowy,
through my thoughts
caught in the here and now.
I won't let her go
until I find someone
who sees me like this
like they did.
Someone who accepts me like that
and gave me the same love
I know that's wrong
I loosen the chains piece by piece.
I can hear yours please
but mine is.
I want you back here.
Just to tell you:
that I miss you
never forget.
and how much it gave me courage
that you loved me

165.
A knight,
pierced with arrows.
is not dead forever
is not gone forever.
memories make him live
there will be stories
through his loved ones.
because he lives on
for the fight he fought.
whether in war,
whether in life
or in love.
'Cause they know
You see him again.
in the realm of light,
full of warmth.
Where he is honored
for his love
to protect those
who live in his heart.
For a safe life.

166.
At night,
on gentle paws,
she creeps through the night.
her appearance,
so different in the day
her eyes light up,
like the gems.
a sight,
who carries a secret.
But what a secret
this being always protects,
so it is robber,
friend and companion.
who can hurt you
and yet loves and protects one.

167.
His love is visible
his love is palpable.
No matter how you are with him.
His faithfulness is an example
he is a companion
in our life.
a howl,
that reaches the stars.
A song,
from forgotten times.
a growl,
that shows his ferocity.
His tooth,
for hunting and catching
to protect
his companion for life.

168.
lying floating in the sea,
the sounds are muffled.
everything drifts away
wave after wave,
from my thoughts
into the deep, wide unknown.
what the sea hides
are not only his secrets,
in the deep.
but also everything bad
what has invaded our minds.
all creatures,
all feelings
what we in us
have hidden.
So don't explore the deep
this uncertain darkness.
You may find creatures
created by others
that pull you down
In one world,
which is not yours
Without light,
full of pain and suffering.

169.
feelings like a storm
nothing sorted,
not to be tamed.
Unknown and yet clearly visible.
I don't know,
what I should do,
to find rest.
Because my thoughts are with you
who is so far away from me.
who is so like me
and yet so different.
gives me strength
to whom I shake hands
when he's on the ground.
just to see one
that he is not in the dark
will be lost.

170.
step by step,
goes with the time.
Like a run in sports
run away from us.
like a marathon
pulls her way away.
what remains
are images of memory.
which overtake us,
at the end of the run,
a target,
on whose life
we can be proud.

171.
envy
the worst feeling.
to want something
what others own.
There are some
take it by force.
It's just not the same
what the others feel.
Because a stolen happiness
is not the same.
So don't envy others
for what they own.
search for the way
to reach your goal.
to achieve your happiness
without hurting others.

172.
Every picture comes up
emerged from deep shadows.
in a sea
from darkness.
it whispers to you
very quiet.
it nourishes the heart
with everything that was.
what caused you pain
times when you were alone
Even the hands on the ears
don't let this whisper stop.
it's all around you
in the dark of the sea.
So let the rays of the sun
also appear in it.
destroy the pictures
to relieve this pain.
let it flow
in its best light.
Look around,
look into this sea of feelings,
what colors it has
what the darkness hides before.

173.
The spring,
once intended to fly.
rose to the sky
caressed clouds very gently.
Detached from his wing tender,
completely unnoticed
is carried away by the wind.
Gently,
almost dancing
travels the world.
Until they someday
falls to the ground.
shining in the sun,
it will be lifted.
to fly again
with ink on paper.
to use your new wings
to bind words
to invent new worlds.

174.
to travel through time
to cover his tracks.
what was to be changed
erase all bad.
Everyone knows the feeling
everyone owns the desire of us.
But who would you be then
if you really can?
would you be the same person
with the same heart
in the here and now?
would you see the world
what is she really like?
Or do you just make it
to please others?
leave time alone
forget that wish.
you would not be the person
who you are today
so don't be so presumptuous.

175.
Time seems to be infinite.
But everything has its time.
It doesn't start at birth
right now
when two hearts unite.
every cell in the body
grows and lives.
every creature
has a goal
what it aspires to.
But what time gives
is life itself
because that is not infinite
but limited.
so enjoy the time
that remains for you on earth.
And do that
what seems right to your heart.

176.
Right and wrong,
does it really exist?
who tells us
that we are doing the right thing?
who tells us
what if we do something wrong?
There are laws that bind us
because the view
what the heart perceives as right or wrong.
is not the same
what another says.
It's not all wrong
usually just another way.
It's not all right
and yet it leads to the goal.
But don't blur the line
as you please.
Because listen to your heart
because it knows
where the border is
it knows,
in what madness
otherwise you lose yourself.

177.
a look over the shoulder,
is not wrong.
Don't look back!
Often admonished.
But if we don't do it
we don't see
what really happened.
Not just the shadows
live there,
and show us the suffering.
Turn around,
have the courage
And also the light
will reveal to you
what you won
what courage you had
in dark times
not to lose you
to find the strength
where you are now.

178.
lying in ruins,
eyes empty.
getting lost in the dark,
the heart empty.
A time,
where the pain reigns.
where one forgets to be happy
there is always this time
don't hide this time
This is a part
how luck comes.
Because somewhere the light breaks
out in the dark.
eyes awakened,
in a shine
of the warmest light.
look up,
see the face of truth.
Accept what she shows you
make the best out of it.
create happiness,
and eliminate suffering.

179.
lost the flute
her sound died.
A child,
which she used
with joy in my heart
played all the songs.
couldn't find her anymore.
But don't forget
is the flute in the heart.
awakens it in the poeple,
lucky,
a smile appears
a melody full of warmth,
unforgettable.

180.
roaming through the forest,
rustling the leaves,
with every step.
the cold of the wind,
heralds the gray time.
the rays of the sun,
roams the colorful canopy,
The world shines in a noble dress,
lets the spirits of the forest dance
before they go to sleep.
So everyone dances in the forest
playing with the leaves
from big to small,
winter is slowly coming.

181.
running,
dancing.
animal and human.
knows this earth
sees this world.
A look that meets
marked with wildness.
are you afraid of each other
even though you look alike.
Even if the language
is not the same.
is this world
our empire.

182.
Dreams,
moving to other worlds.
to find peace
to see new desires.
Still unknown,
when this comes true.
let's wake up
awakens the longing for
what we once saw.
Even if we don't remember
one thing is clear,
our heart knows
knows the desire
who gave birth in a dream.

183.
holding his hands in front of his chest,
almost like a prayer.
whispers a wish
to protect someone else.
not encountered in life
the desire so clear.
Does he achieve by miracles
those uncertain.
Because the ghosts
from nature to companion,
from plant to living being,
carry on the wish.
for it to be fulfilled,
when the wish is so pure
for someone else's happiness
not for oneself to be.

184.
Every word has its effect
like every action its origin.
the word can heal
the words can hurt.
The plot can help
it can also destroy.
think what you say
think what you are doing
don't trade blind
because look
what your heart reveals to you.
what your actions
what the future may change.

185.
shimmering blue,
like heaven.
reflect the light of the sun,
the ghost caught
in another realm.

The darkness,
pulls the body down.
Loneliness tears at the soul
adorned by love and betrayal.

186.
love is fiery
her passion
like a sea of flames.
love is tender
like the soft petals of a rose.
love can create pain
and drag one deep into the darkness.
love can be easy
give a wing
and escape from the darkness.
love is the light
which always gives us hope.

187.
when the clouds
gently pull over you.
the waves of the sea,
gently caress the coast.
This is how the moment works
as if time stood still.
And yet,
changes every moment
So much.
Here where the calm of the moment,
how eternity appears.

188.
a veil of light,
covered the night.
A hand that reaches out to him
As in a dream.
So far away,
long awaited
a memory for eternity.

189.
thoughts of you,
swim in me
along the river,
to the lake of dreams
where I see you again
deep inside me,
wave after wave,
can you reach my light
my center
my heart.
where my love
seems forever.

190.
A soul broken in the dark
are the shards there
faint sparkle,
a light emanates from them.

A little child,
collect shard by shard.
puts together
what belongs together
waiting for someone
and brings everything together with his power.

Although with cracks and wounds,
but as a whole
shining brightly again,
full of hope and love.

191.
a hunger,
gnawing at your soul.
consumes you,
from the inside out.
that awakens your longing
and drops again
until nothing remains
except the hunger for more.
Except the desire and the greed
to feed the dark hole.

192.
seeing is one
listening is important.
Don't understand of course.
Because every property
as important as it seems
learns over time
Joy and suffer.
But how you see something,
how to listen,
how to understand something.
So everyone has a different picture
tries to understand
and see with the heart.

193.
entranced,
torn,
and still in one piece.
But inside you tear
slow and invisible
Do you want your normalcy back?
But what is it?
What does it mean to be normal?
What does it mean to be complete?
When society forces you
to be something
where it is easy
that you are only you.

194.
the shadows we fear
are shadows of our being.
Consisting of fear and failure
that we always get through everything
alone.
So touch your heart
look at the shadow figures
you are yourself
that you fear.
only you can
defeat with your courage.

195.
In your hand a gleaming light,
it crumbles,
piece by piece down,
like the sand.
your own light,
that gets lost in the dark.
waiting for those
who catches it.

196.
with love in my eyes
he looks longingly at the stars.
these recreate her face,
sparkle like that moment
when he last saw her.
a distant memory
forever existing
in the dream he will see her again.

197.
when you lose yourself
there is someone looking for you
when you disappear
feels that
that you're not here anymore
There is always one
standing by your side
like your own shadow
far away and yet so close.
a guard,
a friend,
a protector
who catches you
and fight with you

198.
times make us forget
what we have planned.
Time reveals new things
what we wish for
what we achieve
for which we put our hearts
our blood
and gave our soul.
But the good inside
screams out loud
and bridges the time.
what we set out to do
how we wanted to be
will always be a silent companion.

199.
Laugh and cry,
Joy and suffer.
people who sing
people who write,
those who are silent.
Are we all the same?
It's not our talent
our ability
not the fame that makes us
to be who we are.
our actions,
our words
determine what will happen.

200.
Nothing really has an end
not life
not a story.
Because this will continue to be written,
with time.
Continues,
from human to human,
about joy and sorrow.
The hope is that
what accompanies the story.
for eternity
The life
and guides every being.

© Nicole Klahr

More books:
Shadow & light of soul - poetry of the heart (2020)

Social Media:
facebook: Blackwolfangel.Artworks
twitter: Black_Wolfangel
instagram & Youtube: Blackwolfangel

9 7 9 8 3 5 8 8 1 6 0 3 9